Walks in
Swaledale

by

Geoffrey White

DALESMAN BOOKS
1989

The Dalesman Publishing Company Ltd.,
Clapham, via Lancaster, LA2 8EB

First published 1976

Second edition 1982

Third edition 1986

Fourth edition 1989

© Geoffrey White, 1976, 1989

ISBN: 0 85206 963 4

The author acknowledges with gratitude the assistance given by
Norman Hancock and Geoffrey Green

Cover drawing of Wain Wath Force
by Herbert Rodmell

Printed by Swannack Brown & Co., Ltd., Hull, England.

Contents

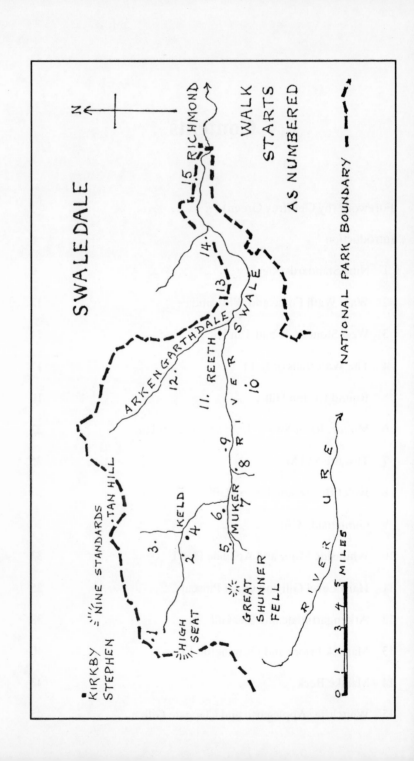

FOREWORD

PLEADING, as I must, special interest — for Swaledale is my nonpareil in Britain — it must then be supposed my standards would be exactlingly high and my taste not easily satisfied. How true, whereby I can say that Geoffrey White passes the test, providing me — a part contributor of course — with a vividly heartening image of the dale and hills I know so well. Within that imaginative achievement his unerring judgement has picked out just those shorter walks which ideally portray the changing moods and aspects of this remotest of Yorkshire dales — rugged and isolated as any narrow valley of a Swiss canton.

Swaledale is made of sterner stuff than its neighbour Wensleydale, but shares a common background in lead and coal mining (in former years), knitting, weaving, sheep and cattle, and good homely Yorkshire fare born of hardy and self-contained indigenous dalesfolk. These people I have come to know over the years, though slowly as must any "stranger"; this knowledge tells me how truly the author has come to terms with his subject, so that he writes from the heart in harmony with the solitary climate of the wild and desolate scenery in and around the area. Nowhere does a dale more aptly reflect the mood of its creator — here the river Swale — swiftest flowing in England, Michael Drayton's "wondrous holy flood," and "The Jordan of England" following baptism therein of tens of thousands by Bishop Paulinus at least 1,300 years ago. Swift is the stream, steep are the roads, rugged are the fells — and the natives match them all.

> O, could I flow like thee, and make thy stream
> My great example, as it is my theme!
> Though deep, yet clear; though gentle, yet not dull;
> Strong without rage; without o'er flowing full.
>
> *(Denham)*

The walks are necessarily selective yet everywhere within the ground covered one is made conscious of the Norse origin — their "Swale" meaning swift; Keld — a spring or stream; Muker — a meadow; Healaugh — a high forest or clearing, and so on. However admirably described and no matter how inspiring the walks, there is a feeling about Swaledale that only visitation can convey. In this spirit I invite you to share Geoffrey White's obvious joys, thereby enriching your own and, I earnestly hope, sensing in some way that mysterious "Something" that is the essence of Swaledale.

Geoffrey Green

INTRODUCTION

THE intention of this book is to introduce Swaledale to the newcomer and to extend the knowledge of the dale to the dales lover. Although many of the walks — all circular — are short it is not difficult to combine two for a full day's walking. Rights-of-way are fully used but on the fells recourse is sometimes taken to make tracks over open country, departure from the public path being stated in the text. Usually, no objection is raised when walkers are obviously careful, but give shooting parties a wide berth!

The delights of the dale — beauty, geology, history and geography — have been praised in many books, but I would especially commend *The Yorkshire Dales National Park* published by Her Majesty's Stationery Office which helps give discerning visitors an understanding of the distinctiveness of the region, past and present. Seeing how the landscape has evolved, they may perhaps come to share some of the concern for it that is held by those who know it well. Another book of great authority is *The Yorkshire Dales,* an Aldine Paperback by Marie Hartley and Joan Ingilby, famous authors who have lived in the Dales for a great number of years and are as familiar with the countryside as any writer living. Knowledge of their chapters on Swaledale and Arkengarthdale adds considerably to the interest of the fifteen walks in this book.

The map for each walk is intended only as a guide, and the reader is strongly recommended to use, in addition, the Ordnance Survey 1:50,000 Maps as follows. Walks Nos. 1, 2, 3, 4, 11 and 12 are on Sheet 92; Nos. 5, 6 and 9 are on Sheets 92 and 98; Nos. 7, 8 and 10 are on Sheet 98; No. 13 is on Sheets 92, 98 and 99; and Nos. 14 and 15 are on Sheets 92 and 99. For the newcomer to make an early selection from the walks it may be of some help if I indicate my favourites at the time of writing (but weather conditions may be an influence, so I am quite prepared to change my mind in other circumstances). Best of all is No. 6 — Muker to Keld. Others are:

	Short	**Longer**
Fell	Walk No. 1	Walk No. 11
Waterfall	Walk No. 4	Walk No. 9
Places of interest	Walk No. 8	Walk No. 15

Muker village (drawn by Geoffrey Green).

What to wear: Strong footwear — my own preference is walking boots for the support they give to the ankles, grip on the ground and resistance to bog; thick socks; warm clothing.

What to carry: Waterproof — preferably an anorak or cagoule; this guide; O.S. maps; compass — chiefly for interest but you may get lost in mist; rucksack; some food, even if it is your intention to return for a meal; a simple first aid kit.

If the weather turns bad, do not hesitate to return by the way you have come. Conditions in the Dales can change very quickly, cloud or snow storms altering the outlook in a matter of minutes.

Swaledale

THE most dramatic approach to Swaledale for the motorist is over the Buttertubs Pass from Hawes in Wensleydale. Pause at the fluted pot holes by the road side — the Buttertubs themselves formed by the action of water on limestone — and survey the picture. Lovely Seat is to the east, across Cliff Gill; Great Shunner Fell to the west — its top hidden by intervening ground. In front is Swaledale head, divided into two parts by Kisdon, impressive in its isolation but only

1,636 feet high, against Rogan's Seat's 2,203 feet, in the mass behind it. Two miles further on brings one to Thwaite and an area stretching to Muker and Gunnerside where, in high summer, old-fashioned wild flowers still abound. In this respect it is similar to the region of Hardraw and Hawes.

The dale does share other similarities with Wensleydale, but it is much narrower and has only one side valley of size — Arkengarthdale; side stream are in gills, not big enough to be called dales. The fells are not influenced to the same extent by the Yordale Series of limestones and are, therefore, not so much in terraces. On the other hand, waterfalls occur in equal abundance. As with Wensleydale, it is the walker of the Pennine Way who meets the finest downdale prospect, this time from a beacon on Great Shunner Fell; the motorist, however, may take in the scene in reverse from the narrow road on Whitaside Moor between Askrigg and Healaugh.

So much for upper Swaledale. An introduction to the lower dale is best effected by first visiting Richmond — a historic town of beauty and character. Walk round the terrace below the castle walls, then ride to Reeth through the wooded gorge. The colouring of the trees in autumn sunlight must be seen to be believed. An approach to the dale not so well known is along the straight tank road to Halfpenny House, reached from Catterick village (on the old Great North Road) or from Patrick Brompton, near Bedale. It goes over Hauxwell and Barden Moors, handy for Catterick Camp. Not only is the route a quick one, but it gives a comprehensive view of Wensleydale and Swaledale together.

The high ground above both dales has been extensively mined from Roman times. In Swaledale particularly (and Arkengarthdale) lead mining has left its mark in the form of desert wastes, and whereas the resultant scene on open moor may be one of desolation, the gills and gullies have often been enhanced by the scars and shapes left by the excavations — enhanced, that is, for those who love wild places. Those with imagination are able to visualise the activites of the past — especially the eighteenth and nineteenth centuries. The miners have left behind old roads and tracks of great worth to present-day walkers. Good use has been made of many of them in this book.

Upper Swaledale has long been a walker's paradise, vying in popularity with upper Wharfedale. The hospitality of the inhabitants is legendary. I have pleasant recollections of happy days between the wars based on the Muker home of Mr. and Mrs. David Harker, both, alas, now dead. Geoffrey Green, my walking companion on all the walks in this book — and very many others — knew their home even better. The hospitable traditions set by them, and hundreds more dalesfolk, still go on. May the reader enjoy — and have similar opportunities to remember — such happy days in so rich a setting.

1.   Nine Standards Rigg

5 1/2 miles

THE head of Swaledale is often regarded as being the National Park boundary on the narrow road from Keld to Kirkby Stephen — although, strictly, the name of the top four miles is Birkdale. The Swale itself is formed at the confluence of Birkdale Beck and Great Sleddale Beck, both seen on the left when motoring from Keld to Kirkby Stephen. The streams are fed from the amphitheatre, seen on the left also, of Great Shunner Fell, Hugh Seat and High Seat — a wild, hagg-ridden (peat haggs) area.

Today's journey is, however, to be on the ridge to the north of the road with two objects in mind: first to see as far north and north-west as possible from the boundary of the area covered by this volume; secondly to visit the curious Nine Standards, a point of call on two long distance walks — the Mallerstang Marathon and A Coast to Coast Walk. A. Wainwright, in his book on the latter walk, has the following to say: "There are many theories about the origin of the group of cairns long known as the Nine Standards, as is usually the case when the truth is not known. Certainly they are very old, appearing on 18th century maps and giving their name to the hill they adorn. They have multiplied slowly, visitors in more recent times having added a few more. They occupy a commanding position overlooking the Eden Valley, this giving rise to the legend that they were built to give the marauding Scots the impression that an English army was encamped here. More likely they were boundary cairns (the county boundary formerly passed through them) or beacons. Harder to believe is the theory that the builders were local lads with nothing better to do to pass their time. Whatever their purpose, they were meant to endure, having suffered little from the storms of centuries."

At the top of the motor road, on the North Yorkshire/Cumbria border, is a National Park sign beside a car park. Four hundred yards into Cumbria, the terrain changes from peat to smooth grass. Park here and take the double trail to the north, on the edge of the grassy area. Limestone scars are ahead, on the side of Tailbridge Hill. Pass to the left of a mine shaft, a succession of potholes similar to the Buttertubs (Tailbridge Pots), and a small tarn. The track bends to the right towards a wall and Dukerdale, steep-sided at the top but U-shaped down below. Keeping to the right of the wall, cross the stream on stones; make for the top corner of the wall on a single path.

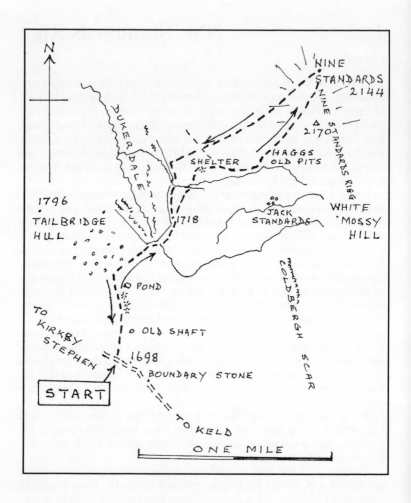

N

NINE
STANDARDS
2144

DUKER DALE

2170

NINE STANDARDS RIGG

SHELTER

HAGGS
OLD PITS

1796
TAILBRIDGE
HILL

1718

JACK
STANDARDS

WHITE
MOSSY
HILL

POND

COLDBERGH SCAR

OLD SHAFT

TO
KIRKBY
STEPHEN

1698

BOUNDARY STONE

START

TO KELD

ONE MILE

Rounding the wall, note two cairns on the skyline. The one on the right is at the edge of a group known as Jack Standards. Make for the left hand one, much lower — it is actually a shelter. A raised path crosses through bog; approaching a cleft, keep well up to avoid marsh; cross two small ravines about 50 yards above the confluence of streams; ascend the hill on a distinct track; pass the shelter; and join the path returning to the stream just crossed, clearly seen up-hill. Leaving the right-of-way, bear left at old coal spoil heaps, dodging through peat haggs on tufts in wet ground.

Once across the haggs, go up-hill leftwards; at the brow of the hill the triangulation pillar (2,170 feet) should be in sight. Although this is slightly higher than the Nine Standards (2,144 feet), the view is no better, so make for the light-coloured nab to the left; avoid some deep haggs by keeping to the left. Soon you will reach a pillar of stones on top of the Rigg — a guide to the Nine Standards which are just beyond, varying in shape and from six to thirteen feet high. Kirkby Stephen should be seen below, and across the lovely Eden valley, Little Fell, Mickle Fell and Cross Fell (in good weather) — the highest in all the Pennines. If clear, the Lakeland Fells should be visible in the west; nearer, to the south-west, beyond Wild Boar Fell, are the Howgill Fells.

To return, walk towards the Howgills on a projection of the line of the Nine Standards, at first on good short grass and moss but later through rough peat. At the edge of the Rigg, make for the cairn on Tailbridge Hill, picking the best route through boggy ground; keep the shelter in sight, passing to the left of it, and on reaching the wall above Dukerdale, turn left on a track now the right-of-way. Cross the stream and, unless you wish to extend the walk to include Tailbridge Hill (for good going and another fine view but carrying no right-of-way), bear left 400 yards beyond the stream, this time keeping to the left of the limestone pavement. The Mallerstang hills are now ahead, the first being High Pike Hill, rising above the point of departure.

2.

Wain Wath Force and Whitsundale

3¹/₂ (or 2) miles

SWALEDALE is noted for its waterfalls and gorges, and this walk takes a sample of each. Half a mile above Keld, park the car fairly near the road junction to Tan Hill and West Stonesdale. Walk down this narrow road to Park Bridge for a glorious view of Wain Wath Force, below Cotterby Scar, and lower falls of the rushing Swale. Start walking up the very steep hill, but leave the road left at the first right-hand bend where a stile leads to a track above the trees and cliffs until, on reaching beech trees, Low Bridge will be seen below. (People wishing to walk only a mile and back from here could find parking space by the road side near this bridge). The top path forks: keep to the right to join the stone track coming up from Low Bridge. Pass one farm; immediately before the second one, Smithy Holme, take a single path on the right, skirting boggy ground. Keep roughly

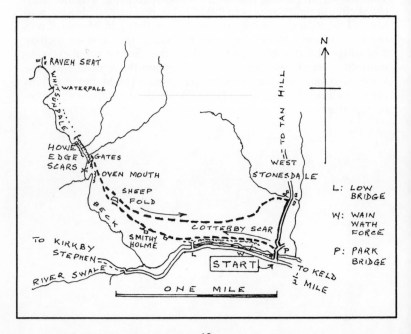

parallel to Whitsundale Beck, now on the left, and pass below a sheep intake on a double track. From here, on a clear day, the cairn on Top of Great Shunner Fell can be seen away back on the left.

The double track leads to a wall at Oven Mouth, where steep crags and a sharp cleft give a fine view of the beck below. Further on, after passing through a gate and another one immediately on the left, there is a great sight of the gorge at Howe Edge Scars. A waterfall tumbles steeply through the trees to join Whitsundale Beck — a beautiful picture, particularly in autumn when the trees are a blaze of colour. This is the ultimate point of the walk, although some may wish to go further to visit a fine waterfall this side of Raven Seat and return on the same track.

Retracing one's steps, this time take the path above the large intake, from which find a single track contouring round the hill, at first towards Smithy Holme, then bearing left and keeping parallel to a wall about 300 yards away to the right. Passing under some power lines, the single track heads towards a barn where another barn is in sight. Keep to the left of both; from the end of the wall a path descends, on the edge of a gulley, to the hamlet of West Stonesdale. Pass through a gate on to the road by the side of telephone and post boxes, and turn right. Now there is a walk of less than a quarter of a mile on the road. Look over the wall on the left for views of West Stonesdale, Swaledale, and Kisdon (1,636 feet) making a fine background to a delectable scene. Go down the steep hill to Park Bridge again for a final sight of the falls.

Swinnergill bridge (drawn by Geoffrey White).

13

3.   West Stonesdale and Tan Hill

9 (or 9¾) miles

ENGLAND'S highest inn, at 1,732 feet, owes it existence to coal, which was mined in the area in the thirteenth century. The last pit to be worked closed down about 1932. The only signs now are old buildings and shafts scattered over the boggy moorland. More facts are given by Marie Hartley and Joan Ingilby in their book *The Yorkshire Dales*.

The chosen start of today's walk is on the narrow road two miles north of Park Bridge, steep in its early stages but offering good wayside parking at Stonesdale Bridge and also a central position — useful for anyone wanting to halve the journey. Alternatively, Keld could be the starting point, but this might present car parking difficulties. There would also be an additional three-quarters of a mile to walk in joining and returning from the route at East Gill Force by taking the path out of the lower end of the village, signposted to Muker, and turning down-hill at the two-way Pennine Way sign.

From Stonesdale Bridge walk up the road for a little more than half a mile; where the road takes a sharp right-hand turn (a sheep fold is straight ahead), bear left along a tractor trail towards a bridge over the stream and another fold, joining a right-of-way at the bridge. Do not cross but go up-stream for 500 yards until you come to a side stream — a turf buttress, surmounted by a boulder, is on the other side. Cross the side beck and turn right, keeping to sheep tracks alongside, to rejoin the road on the right of a conical top, no doubt an old coal spoil heap. Although never far from the road, this last stretch of West Stonesdale gives the impression of eternal solitude.

Turn left, soon to reach the road junction near Tan Hill Inn, to the north of which the Pennine Way goes over flat moorland — Stainmore — to Teesdale and the fells beyond. From the inn, return by the Pennine Way on a wide coal track immediately opposite. Away to the right, more than four miles distant, is Nine Standards Rigg; on a clear day, observe the stickleback end of it — the Nine Standards themselves. Ahead are Lovely Seat, Great Shunner Fell, Hugh Seat and High Seat (from left to right).

Keep to the Pennine Way almost to Keld: it leaves the main track by bearing right to two cairns, becomes a single track by the side of a gully and passes through or skirts some marshy ground. Cross Lad Gill to a cairn above Stonesdale Bridge and keep roughly parallel with Stonesdale Beck, passing two barns together and then a single

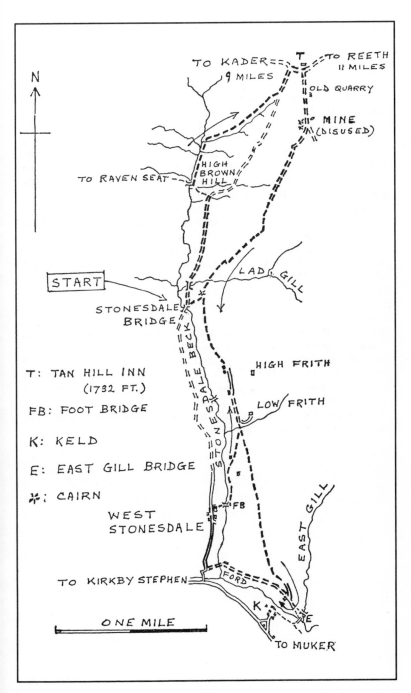

N

TO KADER == T == TO REETH
9 MILES ‖ 1½ MILES
OLD QUARRY

MINE
(DISUSED)

TO RAVEN SEAT — HIGH
BROWN
HILL

LADI GILL

START

STONESDALE
BRIDGE

HIGH FRITH

T: TAN HILL INN
(1732 FT.)

LOW FRITH

FB: FOOT BRIDGE

K: KELD

E: EAST GILL BRIDGE

✳: CAIRN

WEST
STONESDALE

FB

EAST GILL

TO KIRKBY STEPHEN — FORD

K

E

ONE MILE

TO MUKER

STONESDALE BECK

15

barn. Make towards a gate leading to Low Frith Farm, but leave the farm track below the gate and go through a smaller one below it. Soon almost all of the rest of the Pennine Way to be walked today can be seen snaking along the hill side. Pass the hamlet of West Stonesdale on the other side of the valley; Keld then comes into sight, Kisdon rising behind and to the left of it and the tree-clad valley of the Swale further to the left. Every prospect pleases.

The track swiftly descends to a tarmac farmyard, from which the return journey is through the gate on the right on to a good stone farm road, but it is worth going on down the hill for a look at the three stages of East Gill Force. From here, those going to Keld cross the wooden bridge over the main river, bearing right up the lane away from the double Pennine Way signpost.

For the return to Stonesdale Bridge, retrace steps to the tarred farmyard and leave it by the gate to the right of the house. The farm road passes above Catrake Force which can be heard and glimpsed through trees on the left — up the valley is Cotterby Scar. Cross Stonesdale Beck, turn right on reaching the tarmac road and in less than half a mile you come to the tiny hamlet of West Stonesdale, from which there is a track on the right down to a footbridge. Cross it and continue upstream through marshy ground, over two stiles to cross a flat field on the valley floor. Make for the second of two barns adjoining the field and go through a little gate above the building. Take an upward track to the left, sloping towards the wall above, until about a hundred yards before reaching the trees by the side of a gully, go over a step stile. Continuing upwards, the undoubted track of the Pennine Way is rejoined, where soon the gate in the wall below Low Frith will be recognised. Now for a mile go back along the Pennine Way as far as the cairn above Stonesdale Bridge. The track to the left leads to the car.

4.   The Waterfalls of Keld

3¹/₂ (or 1¹/₂) miles

THE finest falls of Swaledale are all within a mile of Keld. They indicate the presence of a resistant band of limestone outcropping on the river bed. Wain Wath Force, Catrake Force and Kisdon Force are on the main river. East Gill Force is the lower end of the side stream, seen from the footbridge below the village. It is so close to Kisdon Force, as the crow flies, as to present difficulty to the cartographer; many people must have seen the side falls thinking they were looking at the major ones, which is a pity, for Kisdon Force is the most impressive of them all. For this reason a chapter is being devoted to a tour of the waterfalls. It must be pointed out, however, that Wain Wath Force is seen on Walk 2; East Gill Force on Walk 6 and, perhaps, 3; Kisdon Force could be visited by an extension of Walk 5; and Catrake Force is at Keld's back door. Undoubtedly the best time is after rain. There is limited parking in the village but no difficulty should be experienced at quiet times of the year in leaving the car in the "square" at the lower end.

Go through the gap at the left of the square into a farm yard at the top of a cliff, at the edge of which Catrake Force is visible through the trees. A stepped path goes down to the falls which come over a ledge on a broad front. Returning to the square, cross the road to signpost "Footpath to Muker," observing, as you go, the lovely setting of this typical Swaledale village, which offers accommodation — including a Youth Hostel on the top road — for the delight of the holiday-maker. Follow the lane to the double Pennine Way signpost where the forward (upward) path is to be followed, through the trees and above the rushing Swale. At a cairn at the top, the Pennine Way track goes off to the right, but keep straight on along a stony path by the side of a wall. Going downhill towards Muker, look for a constructed gap in the wall (not merely broken down) through which a clear track turns back through a field to the cliff edge. The water can be seen in the gorge below; join a path (often muddy) sloping through the trees to Kisdon Force. The water bounds over a small upper fall into a beautiful pool and on to the lower fall — a really magnificent torrent dashing into a gorge and another pool. High limestone cliffs, trees, and clean bare rocks complete the picture. Perhaps some of its charm is its comparative inaccessibility — although, once the route is known, there is not much difficulty in reaching the falls.

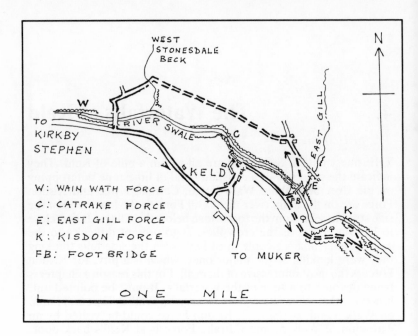

WEST
STONESDALE
BECK

N

TO
KIRKBY
STEPHEN

RIVER SWALE

KELD

EAST GILL

W: WAIN WATH FORCE
C: CATRAKE FORCE
E: EAST GILL FORCE
K: KISDON FORCE
FB: FOOT BRIDGE

TO MUKER

ONE   MILE

Return now to the two-way Pennine Way sign and descend to the footbridge on the right for East Gill Force — three lovely stages of the final moments of the Gill before it joins the Swale. If Wain Wath Force is not to be included in today's itinerary, all that remains is to return to Keld to complete a concentrated one-and-a-half miles of beauty. If the full circuit is intended, head away from East Gill on the Pennine Way as far as the farm and leave the tarmac farmyard on the farm road, by the side of the house. Soon you should hear the sound of Catrake Force down on the left, and perhaps catch a glimpse of its white water. The farm road descends to West Stonesdale Beck and ascends to the road coming down from the hamlet of the same name. Turn left and go down the steep hill to Park Bridge, from which the prospect of Wain Wath Force pleases the eye. The main falls are the furthest away, tumbling below the high cliffs of Cotterby Scar, coming down to the lower falls and a strid-like race before reaching the bridge.

After completing such explorations as appeal to the visitor, walk up to the road junction and turn left. Half a mile of road walking brings one back to the turn down to Keld, surely with a feeling that rarely could one see so much beauty within the compass of a three-and-a-half-mile walk.

5.   Round Kisdon Hill

5¹/₂ miles

TO quote from a National Park notice in Muker: "Kisdon Hill is a
detached outlier from the main uplands to the north and east,
having been isolated by the erosive action of the river Swale, which
has cut a deep gorge to the east of Keld." The hill is the hub of
Upper Swaledale, inviting to be climbed or encircled. Skirted by the
Pennine Way, its popularity has increased in recent years and now
vies with Great Shunner Fell — also on the Pennine Way. The clear
route is signposted from the road uphill from Thwaite.

Park the car on the road side near Thwaite — there is room near
the Hawes (Buttertubs Pass) road junction or in the village itself, if
you intend to patronise the excellent accommodation provided in
this delightful place, typical of the Dale. Walk to the bottom of the
village, below the Kearton Guest House; go through a stile at a
Pennine Way sign and immediately through another stile into a field
on the left. Half-way along the wall on the left (about 100 yards)
pass through a stile and cross a field diagonally to a stile half-way
along the next wall. Thereafter go through fields on a trod, keeping
to the left-hand side (right bank) of the stream called Skeb Skeugh
on the valley floor — sometimes marshy — until, at the last of three
barns, rise only slightly on the left-hand side of a wall. Fifty yards
beyond a stile in a cross wall, there is another stile, this time in the
wall on the right; go through it, turn left, cross a stream and go
forward up-hill towards a barn. Pass to the right of it, continuing in
the same direction to the far corner; go through a gate on to the hard
road and turn right.

Now it is a road walk to Keld, but if there is much traffic then
Angram and Thorns could be short circuited by the use of a field
track on the right. Take the first turning to Keld where, at the lower
end, is a signpost on the right "Footpath to Muker." Follow it to the
first junction, where a Pennine Way sign points to the left and
straight forward. Go straight on. The stony path through trees is a
delight, the sight and sound of crags and rushing water adding to the
pleasure. Climbing, the track becomes grassy — and often muddy
for the next mile; a cairn at the top of the path indicates where to
bear right, going forward on the Pennine Way, below the cliffs seen
ahead. (The left-hand track is to Muker and also to Kisdon Force. If
you wish to incorporate this in today's walk, see Walk 4.)

The upward path leads to a gateway in a wall, where there is a
Pennine Way sign; bear left, keeping to the right of the wall border-
ing a wood below. Muddy conditions have no doubt been the cause

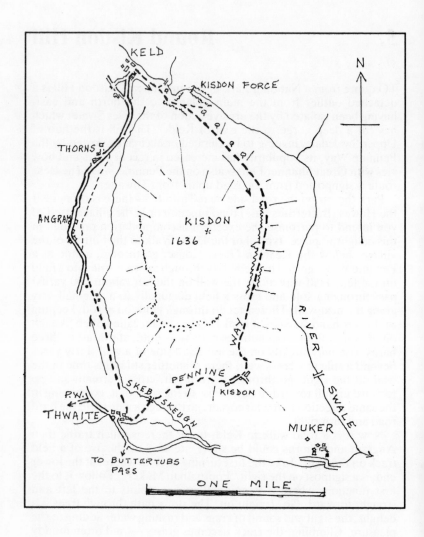

KELD

KISDON FORCE

THORNS

ANGRAM

KISDON
1636

PENNINE WAY

RIVER SWALE

SKEB SKEUGH

KISDON

P.W.
THWAITE

MUKER

TO BUTTERTUBS PASS

N

ONE MILE

of deviations in the path, but it is unmistakable and when it leaves the trees it improves for a while, allowing the walker to see Swaledale below at its best. Passing through a number of stiles, you will soon see Rampsholme Bridge below and Muker to the right of it.

Just beyond an old farm building, another Pennine Way sign indicates a right turn, up-hill, into a lane to Kisdon Farm where a signpost shows still another right turn, along the bottom of a steep grass field, with a wall on the left. Turn left at the next sign, soon to bear right as indicated. Thwaite is now seen below. The wayfarer is amply guided to the beck on a double track across fields, arriving at the trod between Thwaite and Muker. Turn right, where you are asked to walk in single file on the trod back to the village.

Thwaite village (drawn by Geoffrey Green)

6.

Muker, River Swale, Keld and Kisdon Hill

6 miles

IN Swaledale's best walking area, this is the classic walk of the district and must not be missed. Muker offers much accommodation and has been popular with ramblers for generations. Here Richard and Cherry Kearton, the naturalists, went to school — as is proudly proclaimed on plaques on the walls of the school.

Leave the car in or near the village; take the up-hill road past the Mechanics' Institute and keep to the right of the buildings occupied by the grocer's shop. Follow the signposted route (to Gunnerside), a single file paved trod through five fields. At the last field the footbridge over the Swale will be seen on the right, but keep to the track straight forward and return to it by the waterside after going through a stile. This is the well-known Rampsholme Bridge, well constructed for pedestrians. Pools in the river below are tempting for hardy bathers. On the other side, the old coffin road to Gunnerside and the church at Grinton goes upwards to the right, but the route is to the left by the water's edge. The sheep-cropped turf, the enchanting river, the woods and gorge ahead, enclosed by hills, all combine to make a near-paradise.

Straight ahead, on East Stonesdale Moor below some old workings, is Crackpot Hall — no longer occupied because of subsidence — and as one joins a double track which gradually rises on the right, the little conical Beldi Hill adds its features to the scene. The track comes to the edge of a gully, the lower end of Swinnergill with its deep gorge, waterfalls and a footbridge. Cross the bridge or the ford below it and pass old workings. Look across the valley where, on Kisdon, four distinct routes can be seen — the one near the top, beneath the crags, is the Pennine Way. Beyond Kisdon, High Seat comes into sight and below it is Keld.

Rising out of Swinnergill, take the upper of two tracks, keeping to the main track which passes below Crackpot Hall, now out of sight, and also Beldi Hill. The track then passes over the head of a scree through a gate and bears left to a point where the gorge embracing Kisdon Force can be seen — but not the Force itself, being downstream, although its position can be fixed by observation of the two river levels. Continue downhill to pass over East Gill Force on a good bridge. Turn left and enjoy looking at the three stages of the falls before passing over the Swale on a sturdy footbridge. Continue on the track up the hill; turn right at a double Pennine Way sign (you

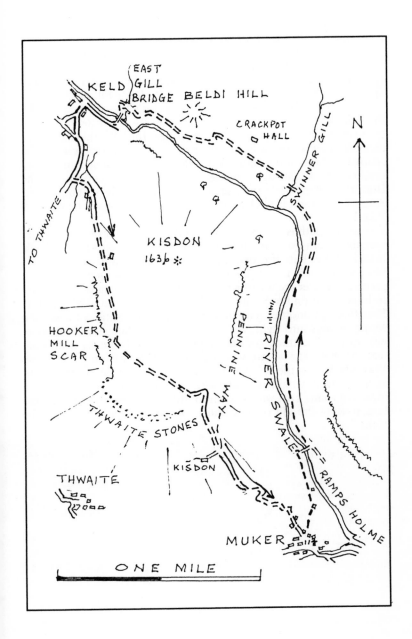

KELD
EAST GILL BRIDGE
BELDI HILL
CRACKPOT HALL
SWINNER GILL
N
TO THWAITE
KISDON
1636 ✳
HOOKER MILL SCAR
PENNINE WAY
RIVER SWALE
THWAITE STONES
THWAITE
KISDON
RAMPS HOLME
MUKER

ONE MILE

23

have been on this famous route for about 300 yards) and go along the sometimes muddy lane for 300 yards to arrive in the square at Keld. (See Walk 4 for Catrake Force).

Turn left in the village, keeping left and turning left at a phone box, and passing the Youth Hostel away on the right — on the top road. Turning left, Kisdon is seen ahead, and the return route slopes upwards on the right of the hill. Pass Hope House Filling Station — once Cat Hole Inn — and take the next turn left off the road, by the side of a barn, on a walled road crossing the little valley and going over the beck on a stone block bridge. Initially, the main track ascends steeply past a barn, through a gate, and below a newly-renovated farm house, after which the up-hill going becomes more gradual. Pass through another gate. In good conditions the Buttertubs Pass road can be seen ahead with Lovely Seat beyond it. Away to the right is High Seat, the nab to the right of it being High Pike Hill.

Now the path is on open moor. Cliffs are in sight but just before reaching them go through two gates, leftwards, into and out of a broad intake. Pass through a grassy lane between broken walls — beware of a hole in the ground — and on to open moor again on a green track over the top of Kisdon (not quite the highest point) soon to look down on the Swale and the route of the outward journey. Pass through another gate and, rounding a bend, all of a sudden Muker comes into sight, with beautiful Swaledale stretching away eastwards. The track goes between walls and becomes somewhat wet. At this stage we are walking one field away from the Pennine Way which is on the left, soon to be joined for a brief moment, but keep going downhill into another enclosed lane to step on to a metalled road. This winds down to Muker, reaching it by way of a lane passing the old rectory and a footpath sign which reads "To Keld."

7.   Thwaite and Muker

3¹/₂ miles

IT is pleasant to walk beside the stream between Thwaite and Muker — known first as Thwaite Beck and then Muker Beck. Ancient footpaths link these two delightful villages, and we shall follow them in this walk. To make a circuit keeping road walking to the minimum, tracks on Muker Side have been included, giving views of Muker with Kisdon and the Swale in the background, followed by the sight of Thwaite and the Kirkby Stephen road to the left of Kisdon and Angram, Swaledale's highest village. But be warned — this part of the walk is recommended only for well-shod walkers or in dry spells of weather, for Muker Side can be very wet.

Motorists arriving in Swaledale from Wensleydale, over the wild but well-surfaced Buttertubs Pass, could park at the junction with the main Dale road just above Thwaite, picking up the route from there. This approach gives the opportunity of stopping the car at the top of the descent to Thwaite, two miles from the village, to examine the Buttertubs — pot holes by the left-hand side of the road.

Otherwise, the starting point is Muker Bridge, near which the car may be left. Leave the road immediately by walking up-hill (but down-dale) on the enclosed green track. After about fifty yards the track takes a right turn, bearing right until it points up the valley; passing a barn, it crosses a stream and steadily rises as far as the lane junction known as Three Loaning End. Level walking takes us to the gully containing Greenseat Beck; cross it on a stone bridge and take a sharp right turn into another enclosed lane going down-hill as far as a gate on the left, opposite a small barn.

Stride across a stream and join a green stony track, between walls, passing to the left of a derelict farm house and a barn. Go through a gate on to open moor; choose the wide gate below (not the narrow one to its right) and keep to the wall on your left. There is a gate in it at the bottom of the field but near it in the cross wall is a stile — go through it and across a footbridge over the beautiful Cliff Beck, cascading down to Scar Houses. The fall on the left is impressive but those below are still more so. To reach them, go through the stile in the wall on the right a few feet away from the stream, and join a single track going down to a stile by the road side. For the best view of the lowest waterfall, it is worthwhile to turn right on the road, but do not go beyond Scar Houses for the road to Thwaite is in the other direction, past the junction with the Hawes (Buttertubs Pass) road.

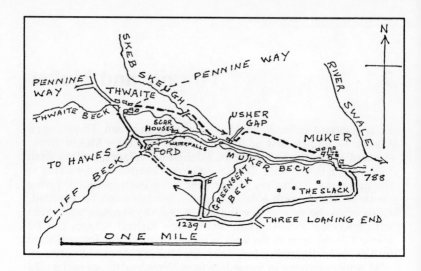

Turn right in Thwaite, going to the far end of the village to follow the direction of a Pennine Way sign to another similar one bearing additional information: "Single file — Highly cultivated land — All dogs on lead." Leave the Pennine Way here (it goes to the left) keeping straight forward on a stone trod, initially by the side of a stream, which at this point is Thwaite Beck. Cross fields by stiles and clear single paths, and pass over the beck — with the peculiar name of Skeb Skeugh — on a sheep bridge. Turn right on the other side of a stile where a notice asks you to "keep to footpath, single file please"; the path returns to the stream side, now Muker Beck, and emerges at the road bridge.

Bear left on the road. A camping club site is in the field between road and beck. At the first farm on the left — Usher Gap — turn into the yard, bearing right to a stile, and in the field at the other side cut diagonally across to the top left-hand corner. Keep to the single track on the left of a wall and on to the west end of Muker.

8.   Ivelet Bridge and Oxnop Gill

3 miles

ON National Park notice boards displayed, with maps, in Muker and Gunnerside appears: "Ivelet Bridge, This fine single span bridge lying just aside from the Gunnerside/Muker road is the reputed haunt of a headless dog whose appearance is locally regarded as an ill omen. More factual is the coffin stone at the north end of the bridge, at which, in former times, weary mourners would rest their burden, while treading the Corpse Way between Muker and Grinton church in the days when Grinton church had to serve the whole of Upper Swaledale."

Not only is the bridge itself worth a visit — do not attempt to go over it in a low slung car — but its setting also is very fine, over rippling river and beside towering trees. Park under the trees and, after admiring the bridge, set off up the steep road alongside the cascading Oxnop Beck. Turn right on the main road and, after less than 200 yards, turn left through a gate opposite a barn. Go uphill through the field, keeping near the beck and observing the waterfalls. Go over a stile in the wire fence ahead and follow a yellow waymarked route which keeps above the line of the private woods. At a yellow-topped isolated post look back for a good view of Gunnerside and Swaledale. Oxnop Hall is down on the right as you continue on the footpath. Marie Hartley and Joan Ingilby tell us that here lived George Kearton, a rumbustious figure, who followed hounds in a pony chaise when he was a hundred, and who died aged 125 in 1764. The house has mullioned windows with ornamental dripstones.

Keep above the trees, skirt meadowland in single file and leave it over a stile in the corner. Continue with a short wall on your left and at the corner where the wall turns away, follow the direction of a yellow arrow across the middle of a rough field, rising to a metal gate beside which on the wall are yellow patches. On the other side is the Askrigg road. Turn left on it and pass a farm building on the other side of a narrow field on the left. Go through the next gate into the field and continue forward diagonally across it. Stride across a stream and turn left to pass through a gap in the wall beside the stream. Go through the next gate in the wall on the right, or a stile beside it, and cross the next field diagonally to a cattle crossing in Stony Gill. Go through a gate in the wall to your right front, turn left and with this wall on your left go to the top end of the field, leaving it through a gap in the same wall near a barn in the next field. Turn right to a gate in the corner of the barn field. Below is Oxnop Gill, with a footbridge over the beck.

Ascend the wide track leading up the other side but do not go as far as the barn round the corner; instead, keep to a clear track beside some barbed wire fencing, above trees, about fifty feet from the beck. On reaching the wall on the right, continue forward to drop down into a depression and go through a stile in the wall on the left. One is in the area of a disused mine, now overgrown but much in evidence. Cross the little valley, bearing left to a small gate in a wall below a barn. The Askrigg road is now seen across the Gill, with Oxnop Side rising above it.

Cross a paddock to a stile. On the other side keep to the right of the wall going forward; this takes you to a stile in the wall on the right. Turn left on the other side, joining a track bearing right on the

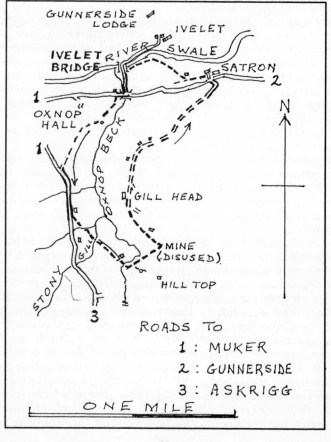

right-hand side of a wall, and pass to the right of Gill Head Farm to join a tarmac road going downhill. On the other side of Swaledale is Gunnerside Lodge, above the hamlet of Ivelet, the shooting lodge belonging to Lord Peel. Many are the disadvantages of walking on hard roads — but this is narrow and the verges are good to walk upon. An advantage is that one may lift one's eyes from one's feet and take in the beauties of the countryside. Here one can see at a single sweep Muker, Satron and Gunnerside; the Swale; and the course of the Corpse Way, of macabre memory but lasting attraction.

Arriving at the main road in the hamlet of Satron, cross it to a "ginnel" immediately opposite, at the bottom end of which are two stiles on the left leading to a paved trod through the field. Follow this path as far as two adjoining stiles, crossing the right-hand one and going diagonally through the next field on a clear single track towards the Swale, soon to be seen flowing quietly below. Bear left for a riverside walk back to Ivelet Bridge, seeing through trees its exquisite proportions and beauty of line.

Ivelet Bridge (drawn by Geoffrey Green)

29

9. Gunnerside Gill

6¹/₂ miles

THE long history of lead mining in Swaledale has been set out in detail in several books. No better example of the remains of mines can be found than in Gunnerside Gill. Mining has retained — even enhanced — in the gills a certain stark and grim beauty, especially for those enchanted by wild places. But on the moors between the gills there is desolation in deserts of stone. Let us, therefore, concentrate this walk wholly in the gill. After passing through stream-side glades of sylvan solitude, now guided by yellow waymarks, we shall emerge into a land of ruined smelt mills, *hushes* — where water from temporary dams was released down a hillside to expose veins of lead ore, and *levels* — tunnels in the valley side to reach the lead underground.

In Gunnerside, find the notice "Public path to Gunnerside Gill" on the east side of the bridge across the road from the Kings Head Inn — the car may be parked on the other side of the stream — and walk up the wide track beside tumbling water. Just before reaching the old school buildings, turn up the narrow lane on the right, then resume progress up the valley. The path passes through woodland above stream level and reaches some old workings almost at the side of the stream. Over a stile in a wire fence, go up-hill to the side of a wall, keeping it on your right and, later, a barbed wire fence on your left, going over a stile where they meet. Keep to the track up-hill from the stream by the side of a wall, pass some spoil heaps and, opposite a ruined building, go over a stile in the wall. The track then slopes upwards, passes to the right of a wall and levels out; leaving the wall, continue up-hill and up-valley on a broad track to cross two little streams in quick succession.

Opposite is Botcher Gill in which waterfalls help to make an attractive picture. Pass below the great blocks of stone making up Swina Bank Scar — at a junction with another track below the scar, the single path ahead may be clearly seen. The scene is fascinating, even though wild, grim and desolate; hushes come into sight with ruined buildings below them and on the other side of the valley. Nevertheless, this is great walking country, with springy turf beneath the feet. Soon we meet Wainwright's *Coast to Coast Walk*,

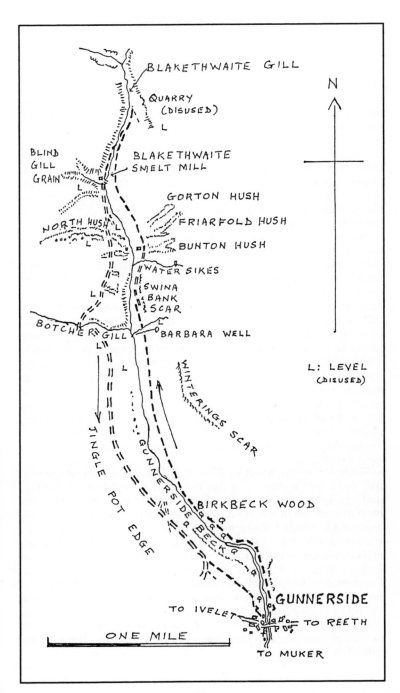

BLAKETHWAITE GILL

QUARRY (DISUSED)

L

N

BLIND GILL GRAIN

BLAKETHWAITE SMELT MILL

GORTON HUSH

FRIARFOLD HUSH

BUNTON HUSH

NORTH HUSH

L

WATER SIKES

SWINA BANK SCAR

BOTCHERY GILL

BARBARA WELL

L

L

WINTERINGS SCAR

JINGLE POT EDGE

GUNNERSIDE BECK

BIRKBECK WOOD

L: LEVEL (DISUSED)

GUNNERSIDE

TO IVELET

TO REETH

ONE MILE

TO MUKER

which comes down the gill and goes up to the right — up Bunton Hush.

Pass to the right of ruined buildings, taking the track forward and upward; at Friarfield Hush we are opposite the impressive North Hush — also on the other side of the gill can be seen the sloping road to be taken on return. Think of the lives led by the thousands of miners in the past — chiefly in the eighteenth and nineteenth centuries; probably walking to work in the black hours, morning and night, often wet through; tunnelling in equally dark and possibly wet conditions through their working hours. Picture carts on the roads seen about you, heavily laden with lead ore, toiling up the slopes. Look below to the Blakethwaite Smelt Mill, seen at the junction of Blakethwaite Gill and Blind Gill (which together form Gunnerside Gill). See the course of the flue in the cliff behind it, reaching the base of a stumpy chimney some 150 feet above the furnaces. Dr. Raistrick tells us that in this flue much of the lead fume was condensed and so saved.

You could descend here for a good stream crossing and an early return. But, for nearer views of Blakethwaite Gill, continue on the good turf track, between heather and stone; observe a fine waterfall near the next ruined building and explore up-stream as much as you will, along the gorge, beneath the cliffs. Returning, find the best crossing of the beck — which should not be difficult unless it is in spate. In any case there is a good bridge to cross at Blakethwaite Smelt Mill, but cross earlier if you can for good views of the waterfall. On the west side a single track goes down to the smelt mill, which merits exploration. In one chamber, the cast iron columns remain in the furnace house. The building nearby, with a fine arch still standing, was the peat store which kept a year's supply of fuel for the furnaces. The high-level, single slab bridge between the buildings is unique. The flue in the cliff may now be examined more closely.

Stride across the water of Blind Gill Grain — a look at the map will show that higher up it has travelled a considerable distance underground — and step out on the miners' track, green now but probably not when it carried tons of lead in years past. Keep to the main track, passing through North Hush on a raised road. Join a wide track which contours round Botcher Gill. Go through a gate and keep stepping out until the road takes a distinct turn to the right; leave it here, striking off to the left across open moor towards Gunnerside Bridge, which should be seen across Swaledale. Sometimes a track will be found, sometimes not, but bear towards the lip of Gunnerside Gill to reach a line of hawthorns. Continue down the hill into a gully to a stile on the left of three renovated houses in Gunnerside. The stile is opposite Barclays Bank by the side of the car park.

10.

Whitaside Moor and Apedale Head

4 miles

THIS excursion affords an opportunity to observe some of the best and most varied of Swaledale's scenery. On one memorable winter's afternoon, when the author and writer of the foreword of this book were in the area, there was a covering of snow on the high ground. Shafts of sunlight picked out Fremington Edge, and pink rimmed clouds gave a fine background to Calver Hill, white and stark. Below, the Swale flowed darkly and the black gash of Gunnerside Gill contrasted with the white hills. Dominating the background was Great Shunner Fell, its top cairn visible at first but soon to be lost behind the nearer Crackpot Moor, topped with a cairn at Blea Barf, 1,772 feet above sea level. Occasional wisps of slow-moving low cloud gradually changed the scene, as did the light from the lowering sun towards the end of the day.

Motoring to the starting point, take the narrow road to Askrigg a mile up the Dale from Healaugh. Climb steadily for a mile-and-a-half until reaching a gate on the left of a sharp bend in the road (when passing an old quarry on the left where a few cars could be parked, there is about a quarter-of-a-mile to go — stop at the first gate on the left). Park on the grass verge and continue up-hill, now on your feet. Alternatively, you may prefer to leave the car further along the road on the open moor.

On the road, cross over two gills and notice a private garage on the left. Turn left off the road on a double stony track just beyond, at first in the direction of a shooting box near the hill top, but soon turning sharply to the left. The track crosses the stream — Crag Sike — and continues alongside it to go through some swampy ground and past some old mines. Cross a stream and pass two heaps of stones on mounds — from here you can see another cairn on the skyline. Pass two more cairns on the way to it; fifty feet before it, turn right and when reaching a gully turn left, to go through a gate in the parish boundary double fence. While you are here, have a look at the round shaft of an old coal mine. It is dangerous but fenced — if you throw a stone down, you will find it is deep. If you wish to continue into Apedale (Wensleydale), take the track to the left beyond the shaft. Otherwise retrace your steps as far as the double cairn, half a mile away.

Continue down the track to a prominent heap of large stones, from which turn off to cross the heather to the right. A right-of-way

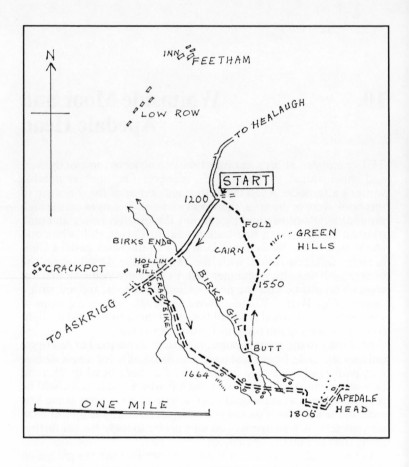

exists here but it is difficult to find a path; soon however, you will reach the steepish side of Birks Gill. Cross the water and make for the shooting butt labelled No 6, picking up a single track in the line of march, not losing height and making for the rough end of Green Hills. An obvious track continues along the top but find your way down to the left on reaching the edge.

In good visibility the hotel at Feetham will be seen on the other side of the Swale. In line with it, at the foot of the scarp, a dark tall cairn should be discerned. Go quickly down, making for the cairn (not to be confused with another cairn which comes into sight on the right at the top of the nab) and pick up sheep tracks continuing towards the hotel. Pass a sheep fold, go through a gate and take a half-left turn in the field to a gate leading to the road and the car.

11.

Hard Level Gill and Great Pinseat

7 (or 6) miles

THIS is another walk to appeal to those who love wild places and, with imagination, can picture the lead mining activities of former centuries. Surrender Bridge may be reached by car from Healaugh, Feetham, or Langthwaite in Arkengarthdale. The roads are tarmac but narrow, and there are steep hills to contend with on the Feetham and Langthwaite roads. Assuming the Healaugh road is chosen, take the road signposted to Kearton at the top end of the village for two miles of lovely views up Swaledale on the left and Calver Hill on the right. The well-known bridge is at the junction of several ancient routes. Park the car by the side of the beck, which changes its name every mile or so (lower down it is Barney Beck).

Take the track up-stream on the east side, marked by a notice saying "Public Bridleway." It is stony with cropped-grass verges, capable of taking lorries to a quarry up the gill. The swift but winding stream below has banks of stone waste. The road descends to ruined industrial buildings at stream level; keep straight on, to the right of the beck and past a working quarry. Climb up-hill to a cattle grid, passing Level House Bridge down on your left — it leads to the famous disused Old Gang lead mines. Keep straight on, with the stream on your left, now known as Flincher Gill.

The path crosses the stream and bears right to pass to the left of an old *level*. It crosses the stream again, passes through a gate, bears right up the hill and becomes stony and less obvious before winding round some old spoil heaps. You will see on your left a stone wall, to be joined later, but keep on the track and make for a heap of stones on top of the highest spoil heap. Turn off left before reaching this cairn, and leave the right-of-way, stepping over heather to the wall. Walk along the wall side to the triangulation pillar on the other side, 1,914 feet above sea level. Go through a gap in the wall and admire the view of Arkengarthdale below. The narrow, tarred road on the other side of the dale is the Stang road to Barnard Castle. Whaw is in the valley, to the left of it.

Since the first edition of this book was written, the wall near the triangulation pillar has been rebuilt and it may prove to be too much of an obstacle. If so, return to the right-of-way where it passes through the highest spoil heap and continues on the track which turns south-east from the old mines to take a course roughly parallel to Bleaberry Gill about 500 yards from the stream. This track goes

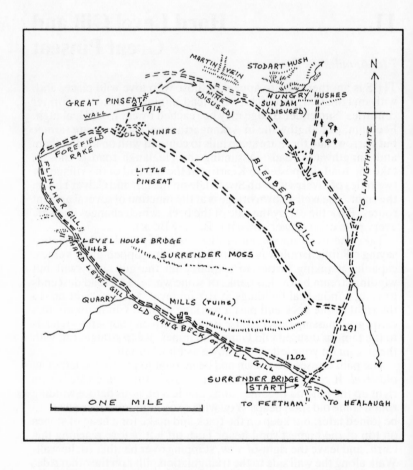

MARTIN VEIN

STODART HUSH

GREAT PINSEAT

MINE (DISUSED)

HUNGRY HUSHES

SUN DAM (DISUSED)

WALL 1914

FOREFIELD RAKE

OLD MINES

FLINCHER GILL

LITTLE PINSEAT

BLEABERRY GILL

TO LANGTHWAITE

LEVEL HOUSE BRIDGE 1463

SURRENDER MOSS

HARD LEVEL GILL

QUARRY

OLD GANG BECK or MILL GILL

MILLS (RUINS)

1291

1202

SURRENDER BRIDGE
START

TO FEETHAM

TO HEALAUGH

N

ONE MILE

36

on for two miles from the mines, joining the Langthwaite/Healaugh road. Turn right for the car little more than half a mile along the road.

For those continuing on the original route from the trig point there is more heather to cross — to reach the moor edge in direct line beyond a prominent spoil heap. Fix your eye on some shorter grass at the lip; you could avoid some heather-hopping by using tracks parallel to the wall for about 400 yards, but turn left off these tracks before reaching a wooden hut. Cross some marshy ground to reach the crest and look for a faint double track going right. Join some old mine workings and bear right to go beside a series of spoil heaps, keeping Arkengarthdale in sight on your left.

Another diversion from rights-of-way is now suggested in order to visit the *hushes* on the left, slightly downhill. Exploration is in the hands — or the feet — of the reader, but one suggestion is to see the remains of the Sun Dam, now disused, in a little valley. Cross the top of the ravine on a sheep track leading to Hungry Hushes, explore at will and then make your way up-hill to join a well defined unclassified road. Turn left, keeping to the track as far as a mining complex where the road sweeps to the right to rejoin the right-of-way. Turn left, and left again, past the mine to go steeply downhill by the line of some shooting butts. Bouldershaw House is seen below and you are now looking straight down Arkengarthdale.

At the hard road, turn right. It is now a matter of continuing along the road to the car but on the way you will come down to the attractive Bleaberry Gill at Fore Gill Gate. Here is a picnic area, obviously very popular, where the road crosses the beck on a ford — but a foot-bridge is provided. Continuing along the road brings one back to the point of departure.

12.　　　Arkengarthdale and Slei Gill

4¹/₂ miles

REETH, fully provided with hotel and bed and breakfast accommodation — and a Youth Hostel at nearby Grinton — makes an ideal walking centre. Many rights-of-way enable the visitor to enjoy the riverside, gills and moorland, often on old tracks from mining days, not only in Swaledale but also in Arkengarthdale where we shall go on this walk.

Motoring from Reeth, a pause on Reeth Low Moor is rewarding. Wide verges allow the driver to pull off the road at popular picnic places. Calver Hill is on the immediate left: Arkengarthdale stretches away in front of you. Fremington Edge is across the valley — we shall later be walking to the north of it — and below us are the twin villages of Arkle Town and Langthwaite. Take your fill of the prospect before you; then continue to Arkengarthdale Post Office in Langthwaite, park the car on the wide verge nearby and walk down to the bridge over Arkle Beck. After admiring the quaint village, turn right to follow the beck downstream on a cart road.

The best time for this walk is after rain when the becks are full; now, when the Arkle will be rushing and tumbling by your side, and later, when the waterfalls in Slei Gill will be at their best. Passing a strong metal bridge coming in from Arkle Town, the road immediately turns towards the trees on the left, under which it keeps a course parallel to the stream, one field away.

Now in a delightful woodland walk, the path takes a left fork, leaves the trees to go up-valley, and then takes a right-hand turn to Storthwaite Hall on the other side of Slei Gill. But leave the track at this right turn and go straight forward through a gap in a wall, adjacent to a barn. The intention now is to go up the gill on old mine tracks, keeping fairly close to the stream until it is joined — at a corner — near the top. On the way, cross some boggy land on stones, pass old mines and notice a cairn across the valley, marking Fell End which is at the north-west end of Fremington Edge. After climbing a stile over a barbed wire fence, observe mining desolation ahead; but as the valley narrows fine waterfalls and ledges in the stream bed lend enchantment to the scene. The track reaches the water's edge when the valley narrows; turn the corner for the sight of another noble fall and the head of the gill, where there is more evidence of mining.

Arriving at a gate in a cross wall, notice an old kiln at the junction of two streams. Tracks go below and to the left of it, the left-hand (upper) track being recommended. Cross the side stream where it

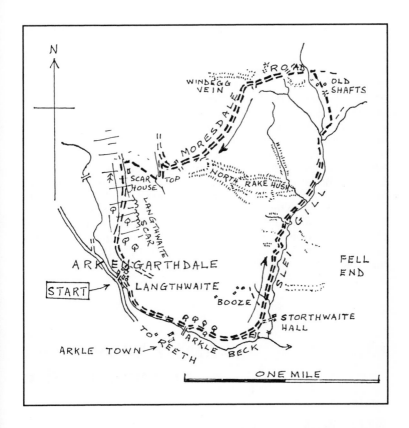

narrows and climbs above the kiln on old slag heaps; then turn left
on a single track through heather and later through bracken. The
right-of-way is shown to follow the main stream on the right, but the
track we are on cuts off a triangle, passing some old pit shafts, now
appearing as hollowed-out hills. A subsidiary stream is on the left.
Join a tractor trail beyond the old pits, upwards through bracken,
and within half a mile take a left turn on a stony, grassy, moorland
road. We are now just below the Moresdale Ridge on Booze Moor,
the track being known as the Moresdale road. Follow it, ignoring
side turnings, to kilns and old workings at the top of the moor,
continuing — now downhill — as far as the moor edge where the
road takes a sharp right turn. Pause to look at what is now revealed.
Arkengarthdale is before you; down on the right is the Stang road to
Barnard Castle — the structure around a cattle grid, painted white,
identifies it.

Leave the road here and turn left on to a Land Rover track, following it for about 250 yards where a wall on the right descends into a cleft. Go down to a small gate and continue down the gully; when emerging on to the cropped grass of the fell side, you should see below another small gate near the right-hand end of a wood and to the left of a sheep fold. Continue down to the gate, turn left, and step out on a green bridleway on the other side of the wall.

Pass through a gate to the right of Scar Top House, now unoccupied, and follow the track gradually downhill to a small wooden gate near the wood edge. Continue in the same direction through the wood, first with a wire fence on the right, then between walls below Langthwaite Scar and on a track through the wood, first with a wire fence on the right, then between walls below Langthwaite Scar and on a track through the open wood until the bottom edge is reached. From here you should see the white-painted C.B. Hotel, then the church and village of Langthwaite. Continue just within the wood as far as a steep, narrow tarmac road (Langthwaite to Booze) and then turn right. You are back in Langthwaite in no time.

13. Marrick Priory and Fremington Edge

6 miles

WALKS beside the river Swale abound in the Reeth/Grinton area. The route now to be described could be joined from Grinton by taking the riverside path from the north end of the bridge, returning by road from High Fremington, adding about half a mile to the journey. Otherwise, the car could be parked at the Marrick Priory junction with the old Richmond road near Low Fremington, or four hundred yards along this single track road, near the river. Continue on foot to Marrick Priory, formerly a house for Benedictine nuns, now used as a residential youth centre. Casual visitors are made welcome.

Less than a hundred yards past the Priory, turn on to a green track upwards towards a gate, through which enter a wood. Immediately you are on the nuns' stone stairs or nuns' causey. The stones all the way through the wood are particularly useful in or after wet weather when the overflow of a stream makes good use of the indentations of the feet of centuries. At the top of the wood, turn round on reaching a gate and stile for a fine view of the Priory and the valley beyond. A long sweep of the Swale is seen below.

The track, now green, continues upwards by the side of the wall you have been following through the wood, crosses a field to a muddy enclosure by a barn — look for a grand prospect of lower Swaledale from here — and enters a lane to pass a chapel on the left and a disused church on the right. It reaches the village of Marrick at a road junction at which a signpost says "Public Footpath to Marrick Priory," which also indicates the route of Wainwright's *Coast to Coast walk*.

Turn left, leaving the village on a narrow tarmac road. Such a surface gives one the opportunity to survey the landscape on the move. Soon, on the right, the Hutton monument comes into sight — erected to the memory of one of the family who lived at Marske Hall — then further to the east two masts near Richmond, near the start of Walk 15. Between the monuments and the masts is the valley of Marske Beck, in the area of Walk 14. The people in the farm house on the right — Nun Cote Nook — must be ideally situated for extensive views of lower Swaledale. The stream in the valley beyond the farm house bears four names all within two miles: Dales Beck, Ellers Beck, North Gill and Oxque Gill. No prizes are offered for the pronunciation of the last name! Before reaching the T-road, Swaledale, with Great Shunner Fell at its head, comes into sight over the wall on the left.

The T-road is the old main road from Richmond to Reeth. Cross it and go through the left hand of two gates, or the narrow slit stile in the wall at the side of it. Go up to the gate ahead which takes you to the right-hand side of the wall going away in front of you — this wall will be with you for the next mile-and-a-half. On sheep-cropped grass, look back for views of the Cleveland and Hambleton Hills and look across Swaledale for the roads out of Grinton for Redmire and Leyburn. The track passes from green turf to heather, leaving the wall slightly and rejoining it near the brow of the hill. Looking over the wall from time to time, first Grinton and Grinton Bridge appear and then Reeth momentarily. All the time up the Dale, Feetham and Low Row villages are in sight. Calver Hill comes into view, shapely and inviting to be climbed, and, rounding a slight bend, you will see Arkengarthdale with Fremington Edge straight ahead.

Still on the right of the wall, pass over some lead mining waste and climb a wooden stile over a cross wall — 300 yards beyond it, our left-hand wall deteriorates and is no longer surmounted by barbed wire. Go through the first gap, cut diagonally forward across to the cliff top and pick up tracks sloping downhill to join the quarry road — stony with cropped grass — descending to the left. Reeth is now to the right and Arkengarthdale behind.

Keep to the main track into the valley. Soon after it becomes enclosed by walls turn left at the first fork. High Fremington and Grinton are straight ahead, but to return to the car through fields take the first narrow lane on the left — indicated by a "Public

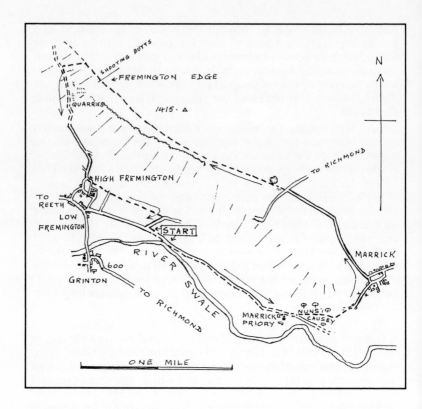

Footpath" sign. The lane soon turns to the right, but leave it here to pass through a stile straight on. Cross a field to the gate and another lane; then cross the lane, pass through a gate, a field and another gate in the line of march. Continue forward, now with a wall on your right and through another gate, the wall this time being on your left. Pass through first a stile in a cross wall and then one in a rebate in the wall on your left; keep in the same direction across the final field to a public footpath sign and the last stile, arriving again at the old Richmond road. Turn right for the car at the corner 200 yards away, or down the road on the left by the riverside.

14.   Marske Beck

6 miles

THIS walk is suitable for most people, being on good surfaces and
using comparatively easy gradients. Marske is a lovely, well-kept
village, lying in delightful surroundings. Beautiful trees, clipped
hedges, formal gardens and cared-for properties combine to delight
the eye. Marske Hall, now in flats, was the home of the Hutton
family, two members of which became archbishops. On a hill to the
south-west is an obelisk known as Hutton's Monument, the grave of
Matthew Hutton (1814). Marske Beck flows through a fine valley,
not big enough to be called a dale in its own right but having all
Swaledale's attributes in miniature. Scoured by the rushing overflow waters from the melting Stainmore Glacier, some ten to thirty-
thousand years ago, it is narrowly confined between a limestone
edge above Limekiln Wood and the steep Telfit Bank which we shall
pass below on the outward journey and above on the return.

The car may be left on the west side of Marske bridge without
giving cause for annoyance to householders, most of whom are on
the other side of the beck. Walk across to the east side taking the
left-hand of two stiles — the one which leads to steps down to the
stream. After only about a hundred yards of stream-side walking,
go through a gate on the right into a field, through which take a
diagonal course upwards towards the fourth telegraph pole. Join a
narrow metalled road at a cattle grid, underneath the crag on
Marske Edge.

Continuing up the valley, pass a group of smart cottages, a
Methodist church and some notable stables — on the site of the
former Clints Hall, now pulled down. After passing another well-
kept house, the rough road enters Clints Wood, soon emerging to
reveal the limestone edge to the right front. The path divides: take
the left fork, pass through a gate and keep straight on. A notice on
this gate reads "Out of Bounds" but do not be deterred, it is to
troops who have a training ground nearby. There is a right of way to
the public on the bridleway ahead. Before reaching the farm ahead
— Orgate — turn down to join a concrete farm road to the stream
which may be crossed either on a metal footbridge or a concrete
cattle bridge. Choose the latter for a sight of Orgate Force,
upstream, a wide waterfall especially impressive after rain.

Join the valley road at some new all-purpose farm buildings. Go
straight ahead on the road, which soon turns to the right to continue
the up-valley trail beneath Telfit Bank — a stony, sandy, slightly

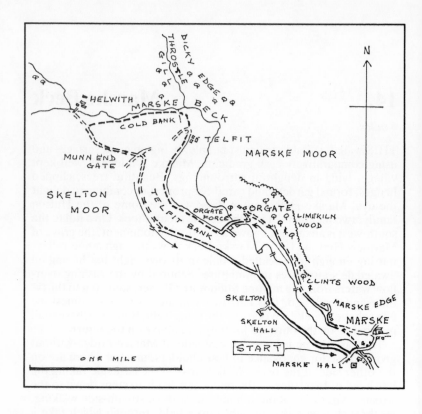

green track, ideal for the walker. Continue on the road past Telfit Farm (i.e. uphill, through a gate). On reaching the first brow of the hill, leave the road which turns sharply left and go through a gate in the wall ahead (the right-of-way here is the subject of a diversion order which will be signposted). Go down the hill on cattle tracks over bumpy ground in the direction of Throstle Gill which can be seen ahead. Near the junction of Throstle Beck with Markse Beck go through a gate in the wall on the left.

On the other side of the gate is a green path through a secluded, serene, steep-sided glade. Eventually, the buildings of Helwith are in sight on the other side of the beck; the path takes one gradually up-hill towards a gate in a far cross wall, but before reaching the distant gate pass through a gap in a broken wall and turn left on a green, stony track coming up from the ford and footbridge below Helwith. The engineered gradient indicates association with lead mining of former centuries. Pause half-way up the hill to look back beyond Helwith to the wooded valley occupied by Holgate Beck which spring from Moresdale Gill in New Forest. It is a pleasing sight.

The track passes through a wall at Munn End Gate and goes over the end of Skelton Moor to the top of Telfit Bank from which there is a fine ridge route home, giving views of the early part of the journey and lower Swaledale beyond. All the time Hutton's Monument is ahead. Passing through a gate, the path continues gradually downhill with a wall on the right; now in an enclosed lane, it is green at first, becoming stony as it steepens. Join a tarmac road and pass through Skelton, the Hall now being partly converted into cottages. At the next junction turn left for Marske bridge.

15.   Whitcliffe, Applegarth and Clapgate Gill

7 (or 6) miles

THE area surrounding Richmond offers so many good walks that it is difficult to select the best representative one for this book. The ancient town itself deserves full exploration with its cobbled market place and streets — some of fine Georgian architecture, some older, solid and quaint. There is a small Georgian theatre, now quite famous. "The Lass of Richmond Hill" — Francis I'Anson — lived here, and the song was adopted by the Green Howards, reminding the listener that their regimental headquarters were at Richmond. Visit the castle and climb to the top of the keep for a well-rewarded small fee. A mile downstream — beyond Station Bridge — is Easby Abbey in peaceful and restful surroundings; it is reached by footpath past the old Grammar School, on this side of the river. Down below is the Swale, rushing and bubbling (a walk on the terrace below the castle walls shows the river at its best). At the foot of Bargate, to the west, is Richmond Bridge, upstream from which is the tree-clad, steep-sided, flat-bottomed dale — the course of the winding Swale. A delightful walk through the woods on the south side of the river starts on the right, immediately after crossing Richmond Bridge.

This walk is, however, to be on the north of the river. Motor out of the town on the main Reeth road, but before leaving the houses — where the main road turns sharply left (at Stockwell's corner) — go straight forward to the avenue of West Fields (an open public park is down on your left). Park the car by the road side where the tarmac finishes — between Whitcliffe and High Leases farms. A notice reads "No through road. Farm only."

Continue on foot past High Leases. On the left across the valley notice Hudswell and the outskirts of Catterick Camp. Go through a metal gate, passing a signpost "Private Woods. Please keep to the public path." The track crosses the top of a field before entering Whitcliffe Wood. Through the trees the river can be seen winding below; then a caravan site and on the skyline ahead, Hutton's Monument, beyond Marske., This is a popular walk on a broad, green, stony track. Emerging from the wood, over a stile, the track continues forward. On the right hand side, on the skyline, can be seen the monument to Willance's Leap— to be visited on the return.

We are now entering the district of Applegarth, the farm on the left being East Applegarth. Do not go down to it — go straight ahead on a green track, through a gateway or over a waymarked stile beside it, and to the right of some modern farm buildings, leaving the field through a gate at the far end and cross a tarmac road. Follow a marked footpath on the left of the road, first through a slit stile. Cross a field to a substantial stile beside a gate. Cross a road and continue in the line of march to a slit stile, also waymarked. Another stile takes you to a large pasture. Keep in the same direction to a stile. Cross a field and a small stream to a gate and to the left of West Applegarth farm and continue on the farm road, which curves to the right under Applegarth Scar.

The pastoral scene between here and Hutton's Monument enchants the eye. Clapgate Beck flows peacefully between fields. Up the valley, towards Clapgate Gill, the fields on the far hillside are terraced, indicating ancient cultivation; on higher ground, woodlands complete the local vista. Marske Hall can be seen, and beyond it the hills of middle Swaledale are in evidence. Across the dale, the rounded How Hill stands out well, although only 825 feet high; between it and Downholme Moor is the Leyburn road.

The farm road emerges on to the old Richmond to Reeth road. Turn right, and for an optional diversion of half a mile each way to a delectable picnic place in Clapgate Gill, pass through a gate on the left less than two hundred yards away. Follow a tractor trail, soon to turn downhill on a single track, and cross a small stream on stones — the main stream of Clapgate Gill is down on the left. Tracks lead through the Gill ahead as far as a cross wall where the right-of-way stops, the reason for which becomes clear on reading red warning signs: "Danger. Ministry of Defence range. Keep out while red flags or lamps are displayed." Just before the cross wall in the wall on the left is a small gate leading to the water side — a splendid place in which to loiter.

Return by the same route to the side stream, from which the right-of-way goes back to the road by way of the gate through which we passed earlier. Turn left and continue up the road, passing the junction to Whashton and Ravensworth. At a dip in the road turn right over a cattle grid beside a notice: "Private road. East and Low Applegarth. Footpath only." Almost immediately turn left off the farm road on to a green track and walk beside a wall on the lip of Deep Dale. In good weather the hills of Wensleydale can be seen over the Swaledale hills, Penhill being particularly prominent. The well-named Deep Dale opens out and we come to the balancing

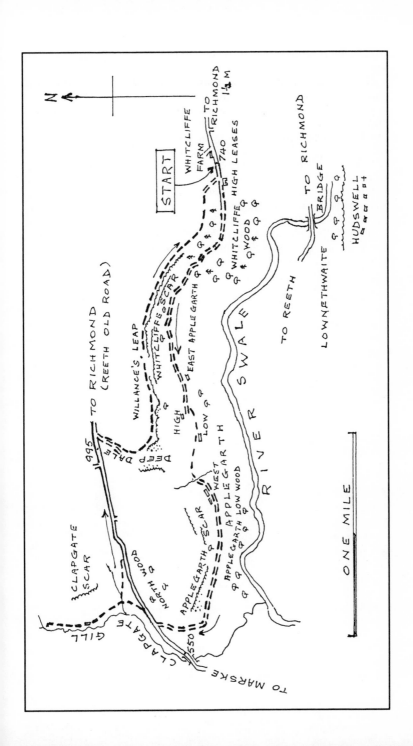

stone seen from below, now observed to be on a man-made wall or kiln.

Now it is pleasant to walk alongside the wall which is above the cliffs of Swaledale, passing above clefts containing junipers and fallen rocks, with no danger to careful walkers. Lower Swaledale and the outward route are seen below. Soon two monuments are reached, erected to the memory of William Willance's leap in 1606 when his horse fell down the cliff but his own life was "miraculously" saved. Continuing between the boundary wall and the steep slope, a point is reached where Lownethwaite Bridge may be seen below. Here cross a stile to walk on the field side of the fence. Eastwards the view is magnificent — across the Vale of Mowbray are the Hambleton and Cleveland hills, and to the south more Pennine hills have come into sight. Breasting the brow of the hill, the keep and towers of Richmond are in view. Go down the hill to rejoin the farm road at High Leases, and turn left for the starting point near Whitcliffe farm.